See You in Istanbul

PERI UNVER

PERI UNVER

ISBN: 978-1484061633
ISBN-13: 1484061632

DEDICATION

I would like to dedicate this work to my family, to
my grandparents who allowed me a peek into their
worlds, and to my parents and my sister Beril.
You inspire me with your love and humor every
day. Thank you especially to my mother for her
immense strength and support always.

PERI UNVER

No matter how many times I've flown this same route I still get painful knots in my stomach. I should be used to it by now. Growing up my family and I would travel to Turkey most summers. I close my eyes sometimes when I am in an airport in Turkey and imagine I am still in the States. I am not really sure why I do that. I wanted to say, "See you in Istanbul" but I never got the chance.

***

I was born with one leg in one place and the other halfway across the world. I guess that's why I am so bow-legged. This could also explain and set the background for my fatal flaw (I like how I say that as if there is just one and not many), because one must always find blame outside of one's self after all.

For this particular fatal flaw I mean simply I want to do everything and not miss out on anything. On a small scale this meant sitting in a restaurant with my family as my older sister, Beril, randomly stated that she could not snap her fingers (we like to blame our genetic difficulties on our parents, but that is a whole different story). I said with enthusiasm, "I can do it!" as I snapped all of my fingers in her face and shimmied in rhythm in a way only Shakira could be proud of. On a grander scale, this flaw meant watching films with adventurers cave-diving and me picturing how I would get there, never mind my incredibly bad knees. In a way this thought process allowed me to venture outside of myself, be curious, and long to explore the places in the world I had been so lucky to be able to travel to when I was younger as well as places I had never been before.

This is a lot of meandering but the reason I always have one foot in one place and dream of another all the while is my family's background. No, it is not the blame game again with my parents. I was born in Fountain Valley, California, which is not too exotic a place. I never felt like a "southern California" or "West Coast" girl, though, because I grew up with tales of rich cultural history, aromatic and hearty home-made recipes, wise familial sayings, and stories of a land that I was able to come to know in person over many a summer. This faraway land is Turkey.

***

On a little street in Izmir, there's a store sign that reads "Unverler." This means "the Unver family" and that shop was once my grandfather's. My Erkan amca (amca means "uncle") took over the shop until he retired a few years ago. Our summer visits to Izmir would include going to that shop to see him. (I cannot even remember what his home looks like to be perfectly honest). I do remember piling into a tiny European car with family members' legs and arms sticking out of the window and at special times even having to lie down, one of the pluses of being the youngest, on top of everyone in the back just for an outing for ice cream. Who knew ice cream, one of the finest creations ever invented, could be so much trouble? Good thing the jandarma (police) are not too strict in that area, but I digress.

It would be so hot that my clothes clung to me and sweat streamed down my forehead and neck. I couldn't muster up enough energy to attempt to wipe it away. We would enter the little shop (which sold home goods) to visit Erkan amca and I would stop in front of one of the fans, moving along with it to catch the fleeting cold air. I came up with a new dance this way, for lack of some creativity calling it the fan dance. It consisted of hunching over a little and bobbing my head to and fro.

Erkan amca would usher us towards the back of the store to sit down, where he would insist on giving us home-made ice cream (some unique flavor like fig usually). Most of the time it was hard to finish but we would because it looked like you did not like it if you did not and could hurt the giver's feelings. There are so many instances of me stuffing my mouth, nodding, and smiling that whatever I was being force-fed was delicious. Most of the time it was delicious, though, so I cannot complain too much.

As we finished our ice cream and my uncle doled out seconds (I tried, and failed, to hide my bowl) I always noticed that his thick mustache was dyed black, along with his hair on his head, and dare I say, his chest hair too that peeped through his button-up shirt. He kind of looked like he was transported out of the 70s, tight jeans and all.

One summer a couple of years ago I spotted the summer house my uncle later built on a hilltop miles away from the main road as were driving by. I do not have fabulous vision but that house could be spotted in the middle of a rainstorm on a dark, cloudy night. It is this bright, not neon exactly, green. Erkan amca had decided to make a private cayhane on the side of the house. A cayhane is a tea house, which shows how important tea is in Turkey. You welcome someone in with tea. On the streets of Izmir all the little shops and eating places have people sitting outside leisurely drinking tea, usually no matter what time of day it is. The two well-known stereotypes about Turkey and Turks is that they drink tea all the time and that they are always late. From my viewpoint, they are both true.

I am not sure if this tops another uncle's (Erturan amca's) house. Usually we blamed things breaking, the garden hose, the shower door, and the screen door (I kid you not) on him. It was my dad, though, who somehow managed to break the pull-chain flusher for the a la Turca toilet in my aunt and uncle's summer home. Maybe it is just me being uptight but I do not understand those bathrooms. Also, why is there no door separating the shower from the toilet and instead just one drain on the floor? Needless to say I had to hold in whatever liquid I had consumed.

Erturan amca's summer house was one of many row houses. The houses were so close together, with only a tiny wall separating them, that if you ate outside it was like you were having a meal with the neighbors without meaning to. At breakfast I felt like I could almost reach over and borrow the salt from the neighbors' table if I wanted to.

We went to the beach that was only a couple of minutes walk away. The water was a beautiful color, like the crayon cerulean, only lighter. I took a couple of steps in and down I went. The beach was deceptive. There was sand for about two steps and then it dropped down into deep water. I laughed when I resurfaced and saw my mom and aunt floundering in the shallow end, the water pushing us fully to the left. I love the ocean but I always have this great fear of sharks, even though I know that there are probably none in the Mediterranean. It is my own fault. When I was about nine years old I saw *Jaws* for the first time. I became obsessed with sharks and then proceeded to watch *Jaws 2*, *3*, and *4*. I could not convince anyone else to watch with me and when a shark burst through an underwater aquarium in the last movie I thought I would never be able to swim again. I should have been more afraid of the sea anemones. Two times I have been stung by them in Turkey. The saddest part is they look so harmless.

***

We were on our way. My older sister, Beril, and I were going to Ephesus. I had heard so much about it. We got up early that morning to catch the tour bus. It was an interesting bunch of people. There was a young couple on their honeymoon, some older couples, a few families of tourists and my sister and myself. The bus had a Turkish man in his forties, heavy-set with a dark mustache (that seemed to upturn at the sides, or maybe that was just my imagination), as our guide who was at the helm with a microphone. He was stating some facts about Turkey but I was distracted by the hills whizzing by. Not listening would get us in trouble later. We finally arrived and got our tickets. We were then led by an older man with white hair on our tour through the famous ancient ruins of Ephesus. Beril had already been there so she was telling me about the Coliseum and the Library. The tour guide was moving a bit slowly. We started taking pictures and getting antsy so we walked away a little from the group. The tour guide became cranky when he saw we were moving ahead of him. It became a battle of the wits when he debated Beril over the history of Ephesus. I was slightly amused and kind of frightened at the same time.

Ephesus was all that I imagined and more. It was breathtaking with all the complex stone work. I was in a place that seemed simply magical. The Library was my favorite part. As I look at photos with me in front of it now it is humbling. I wonder if we should even be stepping so near a part of history, on ancient grounds. I felt small as I passed through that day, like thousands of people have already and will in the future, on ground which has no memory as the wind brushes away any evidence of footsteps. The dust kicked up by my tennis shoes fell back into place almost immediately, as if I had never even been there at all.

On the way back the man with the twirly mustache who conducted the bus tour put on some Turkish music. Beril started dancing and, as we were sitting towards the front of the bus, he spotted her right away. He took her hand and clapped saying, "Dans et!" (which means "Dance!"). He wanted her to dance and Beril, a strong dancer, started shaking her hips and dancing on the bus. I laughed nervously and clapped my hands too along with the rest of the bus but made sure to sit tight. There was no way I was going to be next.

***

Two "sites" or villages lie not too far away from an ancient town named Ildir. The villages are beachside. Along with Izmir and Ankara, this is where most of my father's side of the family resides. Almost every summer I spent there since I was nine or ten years old. The first summer proved memorable as we learned our way around the site and got to know the neighbors.

It is good to know that small-town antics are not just a myth. All Istur and Oytun were missing was a council of elders to decide what direction the villages were to head in (actually I think there is a council of some sort because they later decided to turn the tiny center (more like a patio surrounded by grass and dirt) into a playground for the children. Before all that, though, the center was abandoned and empty. It looked like no one had set foot in it for ages; it had been forgotten. There were also the town gossips as we would learn. Do not forget the misguided, rebellious teenagers either because what would a small town be like without them?

In a short while we went from not knowing anyone to meeting almost everyone. I like to think this is because of that fateful day when my sister and I were to go out with my mom in the stick-shift car. We saw our lives flash before us. My mom did not know how to drive stick-shift and so had to learn fast. By this I mean we jerked into the middle of the town, almost drove into a neighbor's house (the town gossip no less), and then almost ran a couple of people over as they tried to help my mom maneuver out of the mess we had gotten into. That is how we met most of the people living in Oytun and Istur. On the way to the supermarket Migros, a man passing in a car remarked in Turkish, "Madam, it is not a donkey," with a laugh as he drove away. I had no words and my mom, sister and I started giggling. We were unstoppable in that jerky little car. When a tractor honked us from behind trying to pass one day I felt justified in my slight suspicion that my family was special and certain things seemed to happen only to us.

The site cocuklar (kids, or in this case young teenagers) became a big part of our summers there. For some reason they seemed to have the hardest names imaginable. We met a Cagan, an Oguzhan and quite a few Yigits. Whatever happened to good old Ali or Mustafa? Beril and I struggled with the names as the kids tried to correct us every time we said their names. "Ohhlsaaawn?" Come to think of it, maybe they were just getting a kick out of watching us stretch out their names over and over. When Beril and I told my mom that there were three "Eats" in town (we were referring to the name "Yigit") she laughed. We looked confused as she explained that the name we were saying is not a nice name for a person (it means a female dog) and she had wondered why anyone would name their child that until she figured out that we were in fact trying to say "Yigit" (which is pronounced "Yee-eat") which in fact means warrior.

My sister was at the helm as she led the teenagers' soccer team to victory and made them include the girls. She did not like seeing all the girls sitting on the sidelines. Pretty soon that large square of dirt and rubble became an area of excitement. Color me goalie as that is what I became and I put my thighs to good use (just as I had done so many years before in Pee-Wee soccer). The other days we would stay at the beach and just play in the water for hours and hours. I became blond that summer and when I returned to elementary school in the fall my friends assumed I had dyed my hair. Mischief abounded by night as we transformed the town's lonely center into a music-filled game place. Uno was the favorite game, with "Si-kip" not meaning "skip" exactly in English (I did not know this until later). The older teens liked to smoke and get beer from the bakkal (small grocery store) and take it down to the beach at night so no one could see them.

The days were sound-tracked with Kral TV (like MTV but with music videos actually playing) and the nights were colored with one of the town gossips chattering loudly on the phone. This was after she had tried to set her twenty-eight year-old son up with Beril (who was eighteen at the time). He freaked us out one evening while we were passing by on the street and his window up above opened suddenly. He emerged, leaning out of it (like from some cringe-worthy romance novel). Years later he got married to an American woman from New York. His mother liked this very much and even though she could not communicate with her daughter-in-law as she did not know English and the woman did not know Turkish, she conveyed her meaning through varying tones of "Oh my God!" on the phone.

Everything echoed off of the ocean so voices seemed like they were coming from a few feet away when in reality they were quite far. Mosquitoes had their fun. In Turkey you can actually see the mosquitoes as they are huge and loud. They decide to attack just when you are falling asleep and it would not be so bad if they just did not buzz right by your ear. I would wake up and try to find the devilish things. It got a little easier when my dad bought a gadget (one of those made-for-TV things he loves but this one actually works) that is shaped like a small tennis racket and zaps those flying annoyances.

It did not help that I had bad jet lag every single time we traveled to Turkey. It is funny how we do not really change from who we were when we were little. My mother tells me that I would fall asleep during the day while she was holding me when I was four years old and my family was visiting Turkey. I would develop these canker sores all over the inside of my mouth (from exhaustion) and to this day I still get those from stress (lovely I know). I still am the last one to adapt to the time change, sleeping in the middle of the day and staying up practically the whole night. A few summers ago before I was going to be a freshman at Stanford, I went through about ten books as I was sleepless for almost a month. The anxiety and anticipation of becoming a college student and leaving home probably contributed.

***

"Pedin, Perish, Pedish!" was what I heard the first day I met the site cocuklar. I did not turn around, thinking these kids were crazy that first day and decided to walk faster. In Turkish there is a name, Perihan, which I absolutely despise and thank my parents every day for not choosing. Beril knows this and when she wants to provoke me will say "Perihan, could you go get me a Dr. Pepper?"

We spent hours and hours in the sun at the beach everyday and soon my hair turned to the blond it had once been when I was little. We rewrote the hit Turkish summer song, "Uzak Degilim" ("I'm Not Far Away"), to contain the nickname of the boy I liked, "yellow shorts." That seemed easier to say than his real name, Cagan. Singing it we walked to get the famous sakizli (gummy) ice cream that comes in so many delicious flavors (vanilla and chocolate and all the fruits imaginable). I loved that everyone invited you in to tea, that everyone was always late, and that the days passed by in a relaxing blur, a warm haze of memories.

In the nighttime teenagers sang on the beach and hid their bottles of beer. While we walked around the small town a stray dog became attached to my leg and I thought, "This is just ridiculous," as I tried to lose him, only to see him waiting for me on the other side of the beach.

One night when one of our friends in town, my sister, and I were walking the lights in the town went out and we screamed like little girls and ran towards our houses. My mom and our friend's mom were already waiting for us on the lawn with a blanket and snacks. We laid out the whole night staring up at the sky, counting the shooting stars and singing songs softly.

One summer my maternal grandfather came with us. I think of my own semi-awkward social skills and then my grandfather who can begin a conversation with anyone he meets. Beril and I also began recording his memories and tried to start putting together somewhat of a family tree. One day she and I shouted, "No, dede (grandpa), don't open the door!" and in flew a gigantic wasp. My sister, thankfully always the brave one, spent a good half hour trying to get the wasp out of the house while I ran up the stairs and hid. I rolled on the floor laughing hysterically when I watched my grandpa who was confused, Beril swinging a towel at the wasp, and my dad who did not see it and just opened the door to go outside, taking it with him. Beril said, "Thanks for helping," to me but I could not answer because I was still crying and laughing.

***

I still think that maybe the most important thing to remember when traveling is to blink a snapshot of the places you visit in your mind so later you can be that obnoxious person who spots them out in movies and says to the entire theater, "I've been there!" Besides just taking snapshots in my mind I made sure not to go anywhere without my camera.

***

She could hear her funeral music playing as her procession marched her to the sea. She gave in and let them lead the way. Her flip flops glided over the slippery moss on the stub of a dock as her new acquaintances held both her arms in order for her to steady herself. Those yellow swimming trunks caught her attention. She was thirteen years old when he opened his hand to reveal to her a spiky, fuchsia sea urchin and the world. It was summer, his name was Cagan, and her family was new to the little town in Turkey. Her sister told her when she returned later that day, "See, it wasn't so bad!" and her head was a ball of weightlessness and clouds. The hit summer song soon was rephrased to contain the words "yellow shorts." He was as much defined by the sun, salt, and sea as she was. Aggravated, she glanced away from Tolga, who was smirking and kicking sand up on her feet. "Stop it, abi (brother)," was all it took for Cagan to say. The days were careless, but that was before the AKP (the ruling Justice Party) had taken a full stronghold of power pushing the pendulum of the country in a completely new direction and before the Iraq War had begun. Although she would look for him in the years ahead nothing was ever quite like that summer.

***

Izmir is home to me. It is where my dad was born and grew up with his family. Most of his family still lives there. My sister and I would walk from our grandparents' apartment house to get ice cream and I would watch the children that were about my age playing below the balcony with the tiny stray kittens. Beril put her headphones on our grandmother one time to listen (this was before the sleek iPod earphones) and she was shocked to hear the music coming through them. Pretty soon she was bobbing along. That is one of my favorite photographs, her smiling with the big headphones on.

A favorite memory of our elderly grandfather from that time was when we would all rush to use the restroom before he made his way to it from the living room. Everyone had showered by the time he got there. We could hear our grandmother say with a laugh, "Stop counting the ants on your way" ("Karincalari sayip durma").

It was different than another summer when we went to Bodrum and Marmaris (popular vacation areas where young people like to go because of the party scene and beautiful beaches). We stayed in hotels where a couple of funny memories happened around the pool. There was a topless woman who became a staple at the pool and as I was really little (I think about six) I was astonished. I kept pestering Beril and asking her why did the woman not wear a top? Then one day we got stuck in the elevator after returning from the pool. I was explaining to Beril that the topless woman could not understand me because I knew for a fact she was French and of course did not speak English. We were about to go up in the elevator when a woman asked us to hold the door open for her in English. The topless woman was not in fact French it turns out but Australian. Luckily she was good-humored. We then got stuck in the elevator for about ten minutes. That is probably on the list of my most awkward moments.

My mom decided she liked the little tiny jam and butter ceramic holders at the continental breakfast and decided to sneak them into her purse all the while being completely obvious as she looked around to make sure no one was looking. Beril and I pretended we did not know the woman sitting across from us. Years later at a different poolside lounge in Ilica we saw Rober Hatemo (a famous Turkish pop singer). He was lying unsuspectingly by the pool in his tiny turquoise swim shorts with his matching turquoise earring in one ear. Next to him was a male friend in matching tiny orange shorts. Beril and I mustered up the courage to ask him for his autograph but sadly he was quite the diva. That disappointment when you get a chance to meet someone famous in the U.S. and they turn out to be not incredibly friendly is no different in Turkey. He looked miffed as he scratched out a signature on our piece of scrap paper. I am not sure where that paper is now but I will never forget when we returned to our chairs and saw him remove his tiny shorts to reveal an even tinier Speedo of the same color. Speedos, unfortunately, are somewhat popular in Turkey. Not to be rude, but if I had any power I would mandate a ban on Speedos, pass out tweezers to some of the men, as well as deodorant for all on public transit. Saving the world one small step at a time.

***

I used to be afraid to speak Turkish when I was little. Merely letting the words come out just seemed so daunting. Because of sheer shyness and fear of failing I developed my own way of communicating with nods and smiles. Nod once for "It's so good to see you. Yes, it has been forever!" Nod twice for "The weather is great. No, I couldn't eat another spoonful." When I was little those nods and smiles were accepted and thought of as cute. They were enough. I could get away with not speaking. Pretty soon, though, I could not hide. I was afraid of even the most harmless joke about my pronunciation. I could not get the sounds of those vowels right. "Kopek" (dog) and "borek" (Turkish pastry) became my worst nightmares and were dragged out to sound like "Keeerpeck" and "Brrr-deck." Cocuklar (kids) had a good time making fun of the way I spoke. Instead of having a sense of humor about it I withdrew and became defensive. Beril was a great older sister and always defended me when anyone asked why I could not speak Turkish well by saying that I was reserved and understood everything. Now I see that saying "Sivri sinekleri yedim" instead of "Sivri sinekler beni yediler" ("I ate mosquitoes" instead of "Mosquitoes ate me") is pretty funny. It is said that children are able to pick up languages much faster than adults but I think I have somewhat outgrown my fear of speaking Turkish as I have gotten older. Out of embarrassment from saying "I miss you guys and I love you so much" to my family at college, I started speaking Turkish on the phone. It also works when someone next to you in line at Starbucks is doing something annoying.

***

It is funny how there are also some words in Turkish that do not translate into English completely. There are many words for different kinds of love (familial, friendship, lust) for instance, when we just have one word, "love," in English. There some things also lost in translation. My maternal grandmother had many quirky and memorable sayings. These often come to mind in certain situations. One of my favorites is the one roughly translated as "Don't tell how many hairs you have on your back to everyone." This means do not reveal everything about yourself right away to a stranger. Another one that I like is translated as "The baby who does not cry does not get the pacifier." I take this to mean you must speak up to get what you want. This last saying I just remember because I like the way it sounds: "If you put a beard on a goat it is still a bearded goat." Take from that what you will.

Maybe I am thinking too much. It is not what you say but how you say it after all. I would try so hard to find a Turkish word and translate what I was thinking. My parents were there one summer when we were saying something was "absurd." We asked our extended family how "absurd" translates into Turkish and they responded by saying "absurd" with rounded vowels and an accent, like "abseeeerd." I really should just take any English word and add an accent.

***

My father (who we have called baba, "dad" in Turkish, for so long that dad sounds strange now) loves to cook. He is a true master chef, lighting up whenever we ask for a special dish. His brow sweats in concentration as he moves around the kitchen, seamlessly creating delicious, aromatic concoctions. It is easy to see how much he truly enjoys cooking.

I never had the experience of a bad home-cooked meal. When friends at Stanford liked the dining hall food better and said they would miss it during the holiday break I gasped. I would return looking quite well-fed and lament the jeans that would no longer zip.

It is therefore a shame and quite frankly, sad, that I do not know how to cook. Both of my parents put all their love into the food they make (that must have been passed down from generations and stopped with me because not very much love goes into the Velveeta macaroni and cheese I make).

Add one touch love, caring, joy and smidges of laughter and you have food as a part of the Turkish culture. You can expect to be invited over for tea no matter what time of day in Turkey and you will never go hungry (this is as familiar as knowing that if someone says "See you at 8 o'clock" they really mean 10 o'clock). Actually, if you are visiting several family members or different friends expect to be sufficiently stuffed. This kind of giving and warm welcomes never cease to amaze me. This kind of hospitality that is a part of everyday life in Turkey seems rarer in America. I guess sharing is a way of bonding with strangers too. If you enter into a small pastry shop or a family-owned restaurant, of which there are many in Turkey, it is almost like you are entering into that person or family's home. They are eager to welcome you and make you feel comfortable. The sometimes fatalistic Turkish viewpoint is at odds with this kind of warmth and openness. The "It will be what it will be" seems out of place with this kind of social interaction. Maybe it is a way to escape the worries and troubles of everyday life. I would look forward to those long dinners outside during the summer with everyone gathered around the table. I could hear people chatting and laughing, so different from the quiet murmur of the TV news in the background at home. Everyone would eat at the same time and take the time just to see and hear each other. Dinner would last a few hours.

I blame my culinary pickiness on my family for always making such delicious food. I loathe airplane food and TV dinners because my stomach would hate me for it and know I was denying it the good stuff I grew up on. My dad makes a wonderful kofte and pilaf (hamburger meat with spices and a buttery rice) and hunkar begendi (lamb stew with creamy mashed eggplant underneath). I always thought that my dad's kofte and my Turkish aunt's kofte symbolized the difference between America and Turkey in regards to portion size. My dad's kofte is the size of a fist and my aunts' is roughly the size of walnut. Both are scrumptious with all their spices. With my father's I cannot stop at just one but I can pop my aunt's koftes into my mouth like popcorn. One of the saddest moments is when a beloved dish has disappeared but it is hard to remember finishing it so quickly. For instance when you are eating an apple pie and then all of a sudden it is gone (of course I am not speaking from experience or anything, I have just simply heard about this phenomenon). This happened to me in Turkey when one of our family friends made spicy lentil koftes (a vegan-friendly dish). She left them on the counter and then at some point I was alone with them. Sneaking just one turned into a couple and then before I knew it my fingers were grasping at an empty plate.

Back to the pilaf (buttery rice that without bias I can say my father makes the best) for a few seconds (no pun intended). In California my cousins would come over for dinner and it would start with "How are you? I missed you!" and "Hey…guess what? There's pilaf!" By the end of the night someone was bound to steal the huge pot, wrap their arms about it, and laugh mischievously.

My mom's mercimek corba (red lentil soup) would soothe any bit of sickness or sadness. The thick, hot, tomato and red lentil spicy soup reminds me of home and any time it rains, no matter where I am, I long for a bowl.

In Turkey there are many dishes that must not be missed. It is critical, and I mean essential, to try these. These are just some of my personal favorites. Iskender doner is gyro-type of meat (lamb) straight off of the cooking spit served in slices layered with yogurt, tomato sauce, pita bread underneath and a hot butter sauce poured right on top. You can find this dish in most restaurants in most cities in Turkey, including

PERI UNVER

Istanbul, Ankara, and Izmir. Sometimes the best
doner is in hole-in-the-wall type of places. While
walking through one of Izmir's bazaars we ran
across one like this. It was away from the touristy
places and a bit obscure but the doner was
unforgettable. Usually the waiter will ask if you
would like a half-size portion or a full portion and
each time I go through an excruciating debate in
my head. It lasts for what seems like hours with
everyone at the table looking at me annoyed and
hungry and the waiter wondering if I did not
understand the question. Finally, although I know
I probably should not, I usually go with the full
portion. When it comes out and is on a gigantic
plate I think to myself, "This is too much, I will
never finish this." And then, it is all gone. I say,
"Wipe those bemused looks off of your faces." to
my family.

Nothing goes better with Iskender doner
than a cold ayran. Ayran is, bare with me, a
yogurt drink. It may not sound delicious to
everyone but it goes perfectly with the warm
doner. If I am not in the mood for ayran or
heaven forbid the place is out of it, a cold Coca-
Cola goes well too. It is just Cola, no Coca, in
Turkey. Forget about Sprite or Dr. Pepper

though. Dr. Pepper is not well liked because as my dad says, it tastes like black licorice. Sprite is unfathomable. Beril says she once tried to order a Sprite and the waiter did not know what it was. Then her friend ordered a "Sip-rite" and the waiter went to go get it.

Near Ilica and Alicati, in Ildir, Istur Sitesi is a village with a couple of small cafes, a little three-star hotel (Otel Erythrai), and the weekly pazar (farmer's market) on Sundays. There are also a couple of bakkals (small grocery stores). The two cafes are Manzara Café and Turquaz Café. Manzara means "view" and turquaz or turquoise is Turkish blue. The view from the café was of this tiny island with a sand bar that led to the sapphire ocean and one little tree in the middle. Manzara Café was known for its kumru, gozleme, and lokma. Kumru are sandwiches made with gooey cheese, tomatoes, and sucuk (spicy beef pepperoni) served on almond-shaped bread. They are simply never big enough, even when you order the largest, which is called the Yengen (aunt by marriage). I am not sure why it is named after an in-law. Gozleme is flat dough cooked with cheese, potatoes, or meat. Lokma is what I would wait patiently for, dream about, and fight greedy bees over. The bees would begin to circle as soon as the lokma came out. It is basically a fried donut, light and super sweet in a syrupy sauce. Cinnamon tastes fantastic on top. They can come shaped like a normal, round donut or in donut holes. The problem is when they are not eaten hot they are no longer as appetizing, like French fries served cold. The weekly pazars (farmer's market) were fun to explore. This specific one had everything from boncuk (evil eye) bracelets to nuts to all the vegetables and fruits imaginable. These products (not the bracelets) became the night's meal.

An aunt, who also lives in California, makes manti and cig borek and so brings a taste of Turkey to Orange County. These are not easy foods to make as the dough must be rolled and prepared and then the ground beef must be placed inside to boil and fry respectively. Manti is exciting because there are always a couple of uncooked beans hidden inside. Why are uncooked beans so exciting? Whoever finds the bean gets to make a wish. My mother says that when she was young and my great-grandmother would make the manti the beans were really hard and in this way scary to find. I guess a wish is the least someone could get for losing a tooth perhaps. I know one bean equals one wish like a penny in a fountain but nonetheless I pile ten wishes on that poor bean and hope for the best.

Desserts. The word is "stressed" spelled backwards but that it is just an insult to dessert because I never feel stressed while eating desserts, only after when I realize how much I have eaten. For me, personally, lokum, otherwise known as Turkish Delight, is only a delight when the soft chewy candies are brushed with powdered sugar. Rose-water flavor is not a favorite of mine, I must say. They are pretty though, so I can see why the Queen of Narnia offers them to entice her enemies. Actually, Turkish desserts are not my absolute favorite part of the cuisine. I was born with a sweet tooth, my kryptonite. Dancing donuts and cakes, usually chocolate, tease me in my dreams. I got this from my mom as my dad and sister are salties. I would pass up a bag of chips (except maybe cheese and onion) any day for an éclair, a chocolate chip cookie, or a brownie. Turkish desserts are on the whole not too sweet. Cakes there are sad for me as I search for the sweet frosting and chocolate. I do like the syrupy pastries but I must admit I am not a huge fan of baklava. I enjoy the cookies, salty and sweet, but not the way Beril loves one particular Turkish cookie. It is an almond cookie, called aci badem, that my dad works to perfect every time she comes home from Washington, D.C. He will make batches and ask her which one she likes the best.

On the dessert note, Migros (a supermarket chain in Turkey) has a couple of my favorite packaged desserts, Eti Pufs and Top Kek. Eti Pufs are these adorable pygmy-puff sweets (just a marshmallow on a small cookie but with colored sprinkles on top). Top Kek is a tiny, single-portion round cake with caramel or chocolate on the inside. My parents once overdid it with the Top Keks because they know I like them and got me enough to fill my backpack on the trip home. I was tired of them after that for quite a while. Even the potato chips have different flavors there. There are ketchup flavored chips that taste surprisingly good. The hamburgers taste different too, in a good way. I think the spices make it so. Of course the French fries must be paired with mayonnaise, a la francaise (there are quite a few French influences in Turkey, including in the language).

In the summer fresh fish is in demand. In Istanbul there was a truly memorable place that we went to by a lake. It was an out of the way place that was amidst greenery and giant trees. I felt like I had reached a Zen garden with all the waterfalls and ponds everywhere. We ordered trout and it came out in this ceramic plate with mushrooms and tomatoes. I am not a big fan of fish (when I was little I tried to use the excuse that I lived in the water in another lifetime, and I think I half-believed it as well, but my parents would still make me eat it) but this dish melted in my mouth. I felt full and happy until I walked along some of the ponds exploring after our meal and saw the same kind of fish swimming around unsuspectingly. Good thing I did not see that before I ate or I might have had to use my excuse again.

Sometimes my family gets a little too excited when it comes to food. We thought we were being smart one morning and decided to beat the crowd at a popular pide place in Izmir. Pide is like a flat pizza with meat and cheese (eggs can also be ordered on it). We got up at 8 am and drove on down in our bumpy car. When we got there the owner, who we knew by now as we had gone many times for lunch before, was watering down the outside in his boxer shorts. He looked surprised when we pulled up and started with, "Abla…" (a polite term for a female stranger) only to tell us that they were not open yet and to come back at noon. We drove away disheartened that day.

Other times food was cause for fear, mostly at the hands of my paternal aunt, Turkan hala. There was the time my paternal grandmother threw the cherry pit across her patio when she thought no one was looking only to hear it clink as loud as a bomb before skittering off the side to the grass. I have never seen anyone's head whip around as fast as Turkan hala's. There was also the time when my paternal grandfather spilled soup and some dolma on his shirt (bell peppers filled with rice, I like to think of it as a cousin to sarma, grape leaves filled with rice or rice and meat like my mom makes it, do not judge a grape leaf until you have tried it, they are yummy). He whispered to Beril to try and help him get it out before Turkan hala saw. I sense a running theme here. Turkan hala is what I would call a stern and OCD character as we were forced to walk the planks across her lawn so as not to tread on her grass.

***

I had seen Istanbul when I was little. I did not remember it, though, and longed to go back and see the city that had inspired so many pieces of literature and music. The Turkish rock band, Duman (smoke), sing about the city with a certain jadedness and Sertap Erener's "Istanbul" speaks of how the city pulls a person in and spits them out. It seemed like Turkey's New York (Istanbul actually has an even bigger population than New York) with history and artistry all around. My parents brought me to Istanbul before my 19th birthday as a high school graduation gift. I was ecstatic.

We were going to stay with close family friends and they were going to show us around the city. They live in one of those New York type of cool, urban apartments and I knew that I was not going to be let down by my fantasy. It seems wrong to be surprised by the fact that the city was so modern because it has always been that way (westward-leaning if you will) but I was surprised.

I found the dynamic of old versus new, traditional versus progressive, and western versus eastern forces fascinating. One of the most famous mosques in the world, the Blue Mosque, stands erect. The magnificent turquoise and gold-sheen tile work is breathtaking. A great sense of calm comes over me whenever I enter any house of worship. The workmanship is truly astounding.

We explored the vendors on the streets, artists each in their own way, from painters to shoe shines who keep their stations spick and span. We then took a ferry tour on the Bosphorus, which is great as you can see the whole city. The water varies from a light turquoise to a darker cerulean blue. I can cross being in two places at the same time off my bucket list as I stood on the ferry between two Turkish flags, each placed on opposite hilltops on two different continents, Europe and Asia. I am much like the country itself, Eurasian. My maternal grandfather was from the Crimea and after Stalin forced the Tartars from their homeland Turkey claimed them as their own people. My maternal grandmother was from what would be Bulgaria today. My paternal grandfather and grandmother hail from what is now Greece.

My roots are a complex mixture that makes me who I am.

***

In Istanbul we went to the famous Kapili Carsi (ancient Covered Bazaar). It was on a steep hill and I got tired pretty fast. I may have been trudging my feet a bit but I was still taking everything in. There was everything from prayer beads to hand-sewn dolls to ostentatious wedding dresses. There was beautiful framed art and jewelry as well. There were also spices that tickled my nose. Brilliant colors spun in a kaleidoscope fashion and warm scents drifted through the air with each turn. I looked for a Tura and was successful in finding a small silver one. I actually was on a hunt with my mom for something extremely important, something sought after and desired. I was looking for a knock-off Burberry scarf. We scavenged everywhere and went through tons of fabric until...at last! I am not sure what kind of person goes to one of the most well-known covered marketplaces to find a designer knock-off but I can at least pretend not to judge myself (too harshly).

***

"You don't look Muslim." I heard that a few times in high school. I brushed it off as a local public high school/Orange County mentality, but I did feel confused. In my mind I was so above all that closed-mindedness. I had traveled and I knew about different cultures. One does not always look like their religion, surely? Perhaps they thought I was not dark enough to be Middle Eastern because maybe in their mind all Muslims were from the Middle East. Or maybe they expected me to have a head covering if I was Muslim.

In elementary school a girl who was Muslim told me I was not a "good" Muslim because I did not have my arms and legs covered, like her. I remember looking down at my bare legs in my shorts and then up at the hot, bright sun in the sky and asking my parents if that was true when I got home.

We do not eat pork but we also rarely go to a mosque. Something that struck me was in *The Kite Runner* when Amir asks his father how he can drink alcohol and still be Muslim. His father answers that he believes there is only one great sin that man can commit, and that is thievery (in its many forms). When my grandfather passed away, my father told me to say a prayer for him in Turkish. My mother whispered that God hears all prayers, no matter the language (something that she said her mother used to say to her).

No one in my family wears the hijab (on both my mother's and father's sides). In Cesme or just in the small town of Ildir, I have seen some women who are fully covered go in to the ocean with all of their clothes. This never seemed too sanitary to me. More than that, though, with the way water makes clothes cling to every curve I wondered how it was not just easier to wear a plain one-suit bathing suit. Is it not easier to blend in and not attract attention this way? Once, there were three young women that I saw on the beach, a sight that I will probably never forget. One late afternoon In Ildir on the little beach by the dock three neon beings stepped onto the sand with a middle-aged man. Three young women (probably in their twenties) were dressed head to toe in some sort of a neon bodysuit (I had never known they made those) with matching head scarves, slippers, and floaties (I guess they could not swim that well). I was astounded when I saw the bright green, pink, and yellow entities start to enter the water. If I understood the purpose of the hijab correctly it was to not draw attention negatively and signify modesty. I could see these women a mile away. The man they were with looked around protectively as if he were guarding them from some invisible enemy we were not aware of. In between his duties, though, he wasted no time in staring at any young girls that passed by in bikinis without getting scolded by the women he was with. I do not mean to generalize. This is one specific event that I saw myself. My grandmothers used to cover their heads if they were heading into town when they were young. I have my shawl ready when we visit a mosque.

In high school a classmate stated that Muslims do not have the same God as Christians and Jews. I was infuriated and spoke out, which I generally avoided doing. I began to hear more and more on the news about mosques being violated and Korans being burned. It became so that normal, everyday people had to defend their beliefs and religion and explain that Islam means "peace" but fanatics appropriated it for their own purposes.

I guess that girl in elementary school may have been onto something. I am probably far from being a "good" Muslim. I do not know Arabic. Although I am familiar with a few of the lessons in the Koran I have not even read an English translation of it. I can count the number of times I have been to a mosque on both of my hands. My parents were never strict about telling my sister and me what to believe in; they just wanted us to believe in something. I am still finding out exactly what that is. Something that I never thought I would see, though, is becoming afraid to admit that I am Muslim. This is America, after all, land of the free and a land full of diversity. When did that turn into suspicion that our current President was a Muslim? What would have happened if he were?

I would like to read the Koran out of curiosity, just like I would like to read the Bible, and I would like to try and fast during at least one Ramadan. My parents did not allow me to fast when I was younger because they wanted me to focus on my studies.

I am not sure what I believe in. I used to think of myself as more Agnostic than anything but with some recent events I am not even sure if I believe in anything at all. I do know and try to remember that I do not think I have ever felt as at peace as when I was swimming in the Aegean and could hear the sound of the Imam's call to prayers from the distant village or when I had the chance to see the Whirling Dervishes twirl endlessly, hauntingly on a stage in Irvine.

***

The summer after my freshman year at Stanford, I interned in Washington, D.C. for a Democratic Congressman (Bill Delahunt from Massachusetts, now retired) who had quite an affinity for Turkey. He had been there before and loved the people, the food, the atmosphere. That summer I stayed with Beril, who is the Project Manager for a Turkish nonprofit that works closely with Congress. Beril, always outgoing and a social butterfly, has lots of friends. I met many of them, including some of her close Turkish friends. The girls were all driven, smart and pretty. Most of them were single and were not afraid to dole out dating advice. I felt right at home in the valley of the single twenty or thirty-something females in the big city. There were gripes about men, especially those in "this" city (Washington, D.C.) and labels like "immature" and "stupid" were thrown out more than once. I thought there must be something wrong with the men of D.C. if they could not see what they were missing. Then, I started to wonder how much of an effect our upbringings had on us all. My parents taught Beril and me to be independent. They put no restriction on what we could do for the future, as long as we got an education. That somewhat explains my indecisiveness (besides the fact that I am a Virgo on the cusp of Libra). Why couldn't they have just forced me to be a lawyer or a doctor? Thanks for nothing. Maybe our parents taught us to be too self-reliant. That mix of coming from traditional-value families with progressive and feminist ideals in this modern world of online and speed dating seems confusing. One of the girls had lived with her Turkish boyfriend for six years, another was shy and lived alone and had her parents staying with her from Turkey six months out of the year, another did not want her parents to know how serious she was with her boyfriend as she still lived at home, and another's engagement to an American had ended badly after her would-be mother-in-law did not take a liking to her. I could say that there is some difficulty when you are navigating two different worlds and the present time is ever-changing. I cannot say this definitely because I do not know yet and my own naïvete and lack of experience frighten me.

***

There was once a boy who played by the river with all his friends, carefree. He learned to swim there. He laughed often and was even a tad bit rebellious. He loved his home and knew it better than the lines on the palm of his own hand. Then one day a man who was in power cast the young boy and his family out from their homeland. Many, many people were forced from their homes. The young boy and his family trekked miles and miles until they could travel no more, aching for some kind of respite. Finally they made it to a land but instead of refuge imprisonment awaited them. A favorite baby brother was born in the midst of tragedy. Family members were separated, many of whom the young boy never saw again. Finally some troops from a land that would soon become not so foreign came and claimed the young boy, his family, and all of the other refugees as their own people. The young boy and his family lived in Turkey now but his days were no longer carefree. His passport bared the remembrance with a stamp, "Man without a Country." He would never see his homeland again, where he played and grew up. He would meet a beautiful woman who would become his wife and he would see his four children grow up. He would see the land of opportunity and grasp the American Dream that would seem so intangible and out of reach. Those luminescent New York lights and the sight of that bright yellow taxi that he had worked so hard for would reflect in the lines on his face as the years passed by. Dust to dust, earth from the place he never saw again, the Crimea, would touch him one last time through clean, white muslin as the sky disappeared.

Where do whispered prayers go at midnight?

They weave through the air

Tickling   foreign   ears   who   can't
understand them
        Where   do   whispered   prayers   go   at
midnight?
        Do they break through the ceiling, dance
on every breath,
                And traverse the night air to the heavens
                Indiscernible, inaudible, almost indistinct

                        ***

        I shut my eyes tightly against the sunlight
that had encroached its way through the car's back
window.   I am in that in-between state where
sleep just does not come but keeping my eyes
open requires too much effort.
        "Drive a little slower, kizim (daughter),"
my dad says to my older sister in Turkish.
        "Baba (dad), you don't have to tell me
how to drive."
        I sneak a quick peek at my sister.   Her
face looks determined.
        I give up on sleep, so when my dad and
sister are not looking I gaze out my window at the
passing cars and the ocean.   The wind outside
does nothing to calm the intense heat of the day,

but I should be used to that by now. After all, this is not my first summer in Turkey. Something I can never seem to get over, though, is how light blue and striking the ocean is.

I faze out from the conversation in the front of the car. A smell of salt comes from my hair. It is almost entirely blond now from being at the beach for almost the whole day every day. I reposition myself and feel soreness in my right arm from playing catch yesterday with a few of the friends we had made in the town.

I slowly tune back into the conversation and then shut my eyes quickly when I realize it had somehow become about me.

"I just don't understand why she doesn't want to learn the language more. You speak it almost fluently. It would be easier if she tried."
It was quiet after that but I did not dare open my eyes. I work on trying to keep my face as still and expressionless as possible. One thing I cannot control is how flushed my face has become; that always seems to give me away. I wait and hold my breath.

"I think she wants to learn but just holds back. You know how she's pretty reserved at times. She understands really well but it's the speaking that's hard."

After a few minutes, when I am sure the conversation has steered away from me, I relax my shoulders. Maybe I should have said something and let them know that I was not sound asleep in the back seat. I find that there was nothing I could say. Why did my dad ask that? I thought I had done a pretty good job with getting away with not speaking so much of the language. A few years ago I could get away with just nodding my head, but I guess you can get away with anything when you are eight years old.

Why was I so afraid of speaking? I could understand everything but when it came to replying my mouth went dry. Then I remembered the endless corrections of pronunciation, the laughs, and the looks of incomprehension. I felt a hard lump in my throat and swallowed hard.

"Peri, we're here."

I yawn and stretch and get out of the car slowly. We had made it to Migros, the big grocery store. Everything seemed to be a lot faster to get to in southern California.

Someone is gently shaking me. I open my eyes to see my mom and dad with that worry line etched into both their faces.

"Kizim, are you okay? You were sleeping really deeply and we didn't want to wake you but it's time to go."

I look around me and cannot orient myself in a time and place. Then I gaze out the window and remember. Our tour on the Bosphorus is over.

"No, I'm fine, I must have just been more tired than I thought," I say while giving my parents a reassuring smile.

I stay back a little and watch my parents. I feel an immense sense of gratitude for my graduation gift. I had asked to come to Istanbul and they had set up all these activities. I would miss them when I went off to college after this summer, but at least it was only an hour plane ride away. I think back to what seemed like forever ago in the backseat of that car.

"Annecim, Babacim, geliyorum, bekle!" ("Mom, dad, I'm coming, wait!") I laugh as I follow them off the boat.

***

My dad always calmly, wisely, and optimistically says, "Hersey de bi hayir var." This is almost like "There is a reason for everything," or "Every cloud has its silver lining," but it is more like things work out for a reason and in this way it turns out better than you might have even planned. I am not sure if that is always true. It is hard to see sometimes.

I go from being nervous about one to thing to another all the while hoping that this will be the last time I feel the gnawing in the pit of my stomach. First year of college-check. First job-check. Then with quite a bit of fear I realize that the anxious knots will never end, one first time after another, applications that are never done, and responsibilities that cannot be put on the backburner. Life seems to be a string of the small stuff, obligations and opportunities, dips and lifts in the whole length of the line.

Making lists has always been a comfort to me. When I was eight years old my family told me it might be a little extreme to put "shower" on the list. You never know, I think. Thankfully I have never forgotten that, but there have been many more important things that have been lost under the piles and piles of lists in the back of my mind. Sifting through the plans, dreams, and expectations leaves me with the feeling that as soon as I write it down it probably will turn out differently. I find old lists that are no longer relevant, that were off base completely.

On a list, though, everything is in the right place and makes sense, at least on that scrap of paper for a little while. I work through what I have to do that day, two weeks from now, and definitely in the next five years. Even after all this time I am still surprised when I am unable to get through my lists and find that things work out nowhere close to what I had outlined. "If only everything would stick to the list!" I work through rough spots with these lists, using them as sandpaper to make everything smooth again.

My mother finds the little bonfire of sticky notes and gives me disapproving looks. Beril comes up with an idea for something to do and I sneakily fish a notepad out of my purse and scribble it down. "Are you actually writing that down?" "No, I just remembered something, anyway you were saying?" "I still see you," she remarked as I pushed my head into my bag and pretended to search for something while I wrote the next idea down.

These lists do nothing to shift the mishaps, quirks, and certain sense of "unfabulousness" that seems to mark the just over two decades of my existence.

As I get older the lists get more intensive. Now, in place of "shower" they say things like "Possible Majors" and "Applications" and "Possibilities for the future?". I used to have outlines of five and ten-year plans. I wonder where that little girl went; the one in the home videos who sang both the female and male parts of Disney's *Sleeping Beauty* theme song "I Know You," the one who danced around, was fearless and went after what she wanted. I do not think I needed lists then, but it looks like she has been stifled under years of self-censorship and over-thinking, strict, self-imposed standards of what is right and wrong.

This year I learned the invaluable lesson of how overly confident it is to make such definite plans for the future when we have no idea what is in store for us. As I say goodbye to being a teenager and look ahead I realize that the only thing I can really see clearly is right in front of me.

That thing is right now. That is the only thing I know for sure and I do not want to even take that for granted.

***

The summer before I started at Stanford, my parents brought me to Istanbul as my graduation gift. I loved spending time with our family friends who live there. The tour on the Bosphorus left me speechless. The city seemed to be proof of a clash of old and new and the fact that this intriguing push and pull could indeed coexist.

That last summer in Turkey seemed especially important. I was on the verge, saying goodbye to life at home and the safety of growing up and greeting the beginning of adulthood. I was not, and still am not to this day, someone who wanted to leave home. I am that person who constantly misses home. It is like an ache never fully gone. I remember my mom telling me a story from when my older sister was little. She said that she never wanted to grow bigger than her blanket, so when she did my mom sewed fabric onto it to make it longer.

It is this kind of selflessness and thoughtfulness that epitomizes my mother. Not only does she put everyone's wishes and worries before her own, she never thinks of herself at all. Like a small worry doll, every single day she sacrifices herself for even the hope of our happiness as she soaks up all our fears. It is her voice that I carry with me always and her warm embraces are the only comfort that can truly heal. If one day I can grow to be even one tiny fraction of the person she is then I will feel extremely lucky.

**

Her legs twitch with excitement. It makes no difference that the window is jammed, the car is sweating, and my two aunts and uncle, her younger siblings, are squished on top of her lap. My grandmother is in the front seat with her beautifully composed air, perfect, flawlessly clean outfit, and warmth of soft singing and sayings. Beside her is my grandfather with his loud, boisterous laugh and slight cursings up the road as he drives his bright yellow taxi. She cannot wait to see Cape Cod, away from the hurry of New

York City. Her shiny, straight jet black hair falls in front of her glasses. She tries to quiet her bouncy siblings but silently wishes to bounce along. Her father with history embedded in the lines around his eyes finds a parking space in a space that is not meant for parking. Everyone leaps out of the car. What a sight they must have been, in that full yellow taxi cab trekking up the road. It is barely noon but there is already a line to take the ferry to Nantucket Island on that day in August. Her father treats them all to ice cream and the little ones find that the cone is bigger than their hands. She sighs serenely and watches as her chocolate ice cream drops glide gracefully down her cone, arm, and hand onto the ground. The line seems to move at one person an hour but finally they make it onto the ferry. She is free to explore and is determined to get a view from all sides. She shyly tiptoes her way through the groups of people to get a better look. There it is. Across the water all that possibility, anxiety, the little ups and downs of life made from a string of the small stuff. On the drive back home she lays her head against the window and falls asleep dreaming of everything. When they return to their apartment her mother begins cooking and familiar scents tickle and tease her. My mother tells me this story as she folds dough in the kitchen. All the images flash before me, indefinite but clear at the same time. I see this memory for an instant before she tucks it back into the dough before her. Her shiny, straight jet black hair still falls in front of her glasses. People sometimes say that we do not look alike. I see the same straight hair that fails to hold curls or any sort of volume, the reserve and slight awkwardness, and the line of thought between the brows. I also see all that I wished I resembled her for, the self-sacrifice, the quirkiness and humor, and the shine of knowledge and love of learning in her eyes. She motions for me to help and I plunge my hands into the dough to begin.

I was not too far off in my thought of a stoic young girl staring off into the water, wishing and wanting and dreaming. I still see that girl when my mother swims (self-taught) further and further out in the ocean today, and quietly sings a song to herself, taking in all the beauty around her.

***

I am cursed with having normal, loving parents. They taught me the importance of education, being open-minded, and the wonders of the world through travel. My mother and father always wanted me to be successful and even more importantly, happy. Their only fault may have been pushing me to be my best. It is by this way that I play amongst dastardly high standards and live in a world where my biggest critic and worst enemy is myself. I could have just relaxed and led a nice life in low standards and mediocrity. Unfortunately, I have no one to blame for me being problematic and insisting on striving for success but achieving neither that nor happiness the way my parents had always wanted. When my parents say something a thought bubble appears above their heads that only I can read or hear. "Did you get a chance to finish your work?" sounds to me like "You are lazy and never do anything. What's wrong with you and why are you such a failure?" What did you do with my real daughter?" Other innocent comments or questions have the same effect. "Have you been writing, honey?" turns into "You are such a loser (somehow sounds like the way a three year-old would say it with a lisp, "Woser"). You should have had a best-selling novel done by now. What have you been doing with your time?" Another sensitive topic arises with "Are you full? Did you get enough to eat?" spells out "You are such a fatty. My goodness, why aren't you a size 2? You were skinnier when you were younger but everyone your age is still thin. I was so slender when I was your age." My face sometimes glazes over with these translations until my mom says, "Are you okay?" which who knows what that translates into for me.

***

My mother used to always sing around the house. She could take anything said and turn it into a song. We would laugh uncontrollably as I joined her and our voices synchronized in our own off-beat and mostly out-of-tune way. My older sister and dad would call out, "Please, please for the love of all that is good and holy stop singing!", only half-jokingly.
I was so proud when I made it into the school choir in third grade; it took me years later to find out that in order to promote self-confidence at a young age pretty much everyone was admitted.

I sing when there is nothing else to do, or rather nothing else I can do. Belting out a song seems so much more cathartic and constructive than anything else sometimes. It also helps that there seems to be a song that epitomizes every single feeling or situation ever known to man.
I feel the most comfortable when there is no one around to witness what probably sounds like a frightened chipmunk but catch myself unconsciously humming wherever I go. Somehow singing in the shower sounds so much better than anywhere else. It might be something to do with the echoing off of the walls.

One of the most simple, but fondest memories is sitting down with my family after a particularly grueling day at high school and watching the beginning auditions for *American Idol*. This is when you wish that someone had been a good friend and told a hopeful contestant the truth. Suddenly, I feel like the most talented singer alive.

I feel the song stuck in my head, tap my pencil against the desk, and bump my foot against the floor. Before I sing I let the song create a hollow point in my chest that aches. I close my eyes and see myself as the lead singer of an all-male band. I am not sure why the fantasy always consists of an all-male band but it seems quite vivid in my dreams nonetheless.

Singing reminds me of my favorite time in the day, although I never seem to wake up early enough. Still mornings, when everyone is blissfully ignorant of the world around them and the sky is misty and gray, are never around for too long. I hear an Imam call out from the mosque with intermingling strength and vulnerability. I wonder at this and am humbled and saddened at the realization that my singing is so shallow in comparison.

***

The Island: Part One

The water was perfect. The sun was high enough to beat down steadily and make it warm. There were few waves and you could clearly see your toes brush the unassuming yellow sea anemones and avoid the purple, prickly sea urchins. The girl with the curly, auburn hair waited for her little sister as always. She was eight years her senior and felt protective. Her younger sister's constant company was both comforting and irritating at the same time. "Come on, the water's perfect!" She shouted as she went in head-first.

The younger sister took her time tip-toeing in, slowly getting used to the water before starting to swim. She decided not to dunk her head in right away. The older sister waited for the younger one to catch up. They swam for a while, complacently, without saying anything. After a while they had gotten pretty far out. Their house looked small in the distance as they both turned around, treading water. "Let's swim to the island," the older sister said. She had thought of this suddenly and said her thought out loud almost immediately after. She wanted to do something new and have a short adventure for the day. The island did not seem too far and she was determined.

"Isn't it a little far?" The younger one asked, worried.

"No, it shouldn't be too far. Look how far we've come out already! Let's go!"

The older sister led the way and the younger sister followed. It turned out to be a lot farther than they had expected. She saw her younger sister getting a little tired and became worried. "It's not too much farther. We're almost there. Don't look down." She knew without asking or being told that the younger sister was sometimes afraid of the deep waters and frightened herself with her imagination of winding seaweed, sharks, and the like.

They finally made it to the island with just enough strength to plop belly-down on the sandy shore. The warm water lapped soothingly and they glanced around them. She got up to explore but never went too far away from her little sister. She saw the next island in the distance and wondered. She decided the distance to that island would be even farther. Another time, she thought. The two sisters sat a long while and talked about everything, and nothing. They turned back and found that the swim was easier than it had been getting to the island.

She felt good and thought that she had accomplished a big thing for the day. They walked back to the house, the one in the lead without worry and the one following too tired to worry. They soon found that their parents had been really worried and upset. "Why couldn't you have let us know at least where you were going?"

She was not sure if she regretted it. She felt badly about her parents but then decided that not saying anything or telling anyone was the whole point.

***

The Island: Part Two

An island may be a cliché form of metaphor. Still the show *LOST* was hugely successful and I stuck through it for all of the six seasons, only to find that the characters were indeed dead. Across the ocean from the "sites" are two small islands. They seem pretty close. People swim to the closest island and one woman in the "site" swam early every morning like she was training for a marathon.

Beril and I were swimming one day when she said, "Let's swim to the island." Just as simple as that, it was a statement not a question. This is probably a good symbol of our relationship. She is eight years older than me, after all. She leads, I follow, and usually without questions. I am not sure why I did not say "no" or ask her why she wanted to swim to the island so badly that day. When I reflect back on it I actually was not that excited for the swim. I just followed her and when we reached the deep waters it was a good thing she told me to not look down and tried to assuage my fears because that billowy black seaweed below made me want to turn back.

We swam for what seemed like a long time and my arms and legs ached. Beril was, and still is to this day, a better swimmer than me. I can swim but she is a great swimmer. She glides effortlessly through the water and I have a tendency to be lazy as I revert to floating and doggie-paddling. We finally reached the shallow water and sand bar that leads to the island. The island was miniature; it probably could be explored end to end in just a few minutes. She and I lay belly-down on the pebbly sand, me observing the tiny shells. Water splashed us as the sun baked our backs. We stayed for quite a while. She looked off into the distance to observe the other island. It turned out the distance between the two is even further than the distance from the mainland to the island we swam to which was deceiving.

We decided to head back and I dreaded the swim. Fortunately it went by faster than the swim there. When we got out of the water and returned to the house my dad was outside and my mom was preparing lunch. My dad just smiled to himself (which is at times aggravating when no one else is particularly amused). My mom did not talk to us. That was the strangest thing. I have never not spoken to my mom or vice versa. I mean, I get mad at her and everything but to not have her respond to anything we said did not feel good. She was angry we had not told her that we were swimming to the island (of course our defense was it was not premeditated, but I sometimes think that Beril had already thought of it ahead of time). I used to think if it were up to me I would have told my parents since I like to plan everything and that has been ingrained in me, but I realize that I did not even think about it at the time. I felt badly for making her worry. Speedboats pass by the island frequently without watching for swimmers and the tides change when it becomes windy (usually later in the day). Beril did not seem too affected and my suspicions were confirmed years later when she swam to the island again (this time by herself) and failed to mention it to our parents once again. I am starting to think this is not a coincidence.

***

I have no ear for languages. I had taken Spanish in high school, all the while to embarrass myself during the tango (my teacher said, "Move your hips, why are they so stiff?") and to say, "Grass-ee-ass" in class one day without remembering to round my vowels. It had been a late night. I should have picked up Turkish better with summers spent there and hearing family speak it. Why I chose to take Chinese, then, makes no sense whatsoever. I remember David Sedaris sadly trying to learn French in *Me Talk Pretty One Day*. The teacher asks us to repeat after her and we all sort of mumble away to ourselves. All except for that one student who I am convinced has taken Chinese before.

The only way to explain it is that I have these fantasies of going to China. I can see myself there, attempting to use my tiny bit of Chinese. I can ask how you are, how your father's health is, who he or she is, what country you are from, and what your family name is. In short, I am ready for small-talk. Hopefully soon I will learn to ask what today's date is and also what you like to do.

In Chinese class I pray to not be called on, and of course inevitably I always am. This gave way to surprise when I realized my accent and pronunciation were not the worst in the class. After a brutal diagnosis by our teacher (she went one by one around the room to hear our pronunciation in front of the class) two men were told that they would need to come to her office hours. This translated roughly into, "You need help, badly. Please do not embarrass yourself any further." I felt bad when I silently rejoiced. Then I heard the deep sighs of relief that were audible in the class and saw the looks of pity. I guess I was not the only one who thought, "Good grief, thank goodness it wasn't me." I am not sure when I will be able to put the Chinese I have learned into effect, but I enjoy giving my friends who speak Chinese a laugh and my friends who do not speak Chinese a surprise, when I say enthusiastically "Wo le karaoke."

***

PERI UNVER

ABOUT THE AUTHOR

Peri Unver is a student at Stanford University.
She wants to be a writer. On top of travel and
writing, Peri's loves include film and her puppy
Pilgrim. She admires David Sedaris for the way he
is able to utilize humor and still get his family to
talk to him after revealing all of their quirks.

SEE YOU IN INSTANBUL

PERI UNVER

SEE YOU IN INSTANBUL

Made in the USA
San Bernardino, CA
01 June 2013